Answers
The Akashic
Records

A 100-book series of pre-pandemic live group Akashic Record Q&A sessions down-stepped, recorded and transcribed by Aingeal Rose & Ahonu

Book 2 (of 100) includes...

Hitler, Frequencies, Aliens, Entities, GM Crops, US Politics, World Politics, Super Soldiers, Soul Levels, Fracking, Lifetimes, Jesus, Children, The Right Place, & General Questions

https://answersfromtheakashicrecords.com

i

Answers From The
Akashic Records

Series: **Book 2** in the Answers From The Akashic Records Series
O'Grady, Aingeal Rose, 1953–
O'Grady, Kevin (Ahonu), 1958-
Aingeal Rose & Ahonu.
Print ISBN: 9781683230564
eBook ISBN: 9781880765500
Designed and Edited by: Aingeal Rose & Ahonu
From a session on 12 May 2013.
Artwork: AHONU.com
Published by Akashic Records Press,
an imprint of Twin Flame Productions LLC
Printed in the United States of America
All enquiries to the publisher at:
Twin Flame Productions LLC
We Publish Beautiful Books - Yours Can Be One Of Them!
admin@twinflameproductions.us
https://twinflameproductions.us

Author's Note

Many years ago, in the pursuit of spiritual knowledge, we invited people to weekly group sessions to inquire into the Akashic Records to understand our world, our spirituality and our collective purpose. Aingeal Rose had been accessing the Akashic field for over 35 years giving private consultations to people around the world, but as time went by, the need grew to ask bigger questions of Source, not just personal ones. These books are the result. You are reading practical spirituality in a fast-changing world!

You'll find answers to questions about Consciousness, Twin Flames & Soul Mates, Kundalini, Chakras, Gifted Children, Fairies, Healing, Lightbodies, God, Creation, The Future, Inner Earth, Conception, Saints, Longevity, DNA, Marijuana, Free Energy, Famous Deceased, Stress, Prophecies, Prayer, Joy, Christian Sacraments, Alchemy, Dolphins & Whales, Symbolism, What the Trees/Water/Oceans/Sky and the Land has to say.

You will find answers about the Solar System, Crystals, Earth, Evolution, Technology, Luck, Karma, and Planes of Existence After Death.

There are answers about Time, Timelines, Ghosts, Spirits, Multidimensional Selves, Sacred Geometry and more, asked by people from all walks of life all round the world.

This is the time for accelerated advancement and we believe it offers the potential for illumination, joy and blessings. Like us, you may be feeling this quickening, and it is our intention these books help you shift and adjust to the demands of this time. We offer you this information from Source via the Akashic Records and hope you will experience peace, understanding and illumination.

Aingeal Rose & Ahonu
Sedona, AZ.

One of the profound statements in this book:

Negative forces have no power of their own,
but get their power from being fed negative
thoughts, feelings and fears by us.
So, when you're in stark terror,
it's hard to believe that some part of you
is choosing it instead of peace,
but this is, in fact, the case!

We dedicate this book to all our overcoming,
to our consistently choosing peace.

Table of Contents

Introduction

About The Akashic Records

The Akashic Records is a *'place'* in spirit, a vast library, where the events of creation and everything in it is recorded. Everyone has access to the Akashic Records where all these answers are held if they are able to tune into them. The Records are a field of knowledge about creation and the movement of our lives. This is why we felt it was the perfect place to look for the answers to humanity's questions.

We surprised ourselves at the amount of profound content in the form of video, audio and transcripts we've collected from our many conversations with Source in the Akashic Records. So, if you have been confused, unsure, uncertain, or just plain curious about life and the Earth—you will find many answers here. Indeed, in this 100-book series (in 10 volume sets) of print, ebook and audio books alone, we have 100 completed sessions in the Akashic library to date!

Each session was between 1-1½ hours when recorded, making the collection at the moment over 120 hours of deep, loving, life-changing content! Each session contains an average of 40 profound statements from the Akashic Records, bringing the total number of statements to over 4,000!

We believe this is one of the largest collections of Akashic Records content in the world, and we are grateful to be able to offer this information to you during this major time of change on Earth.

Remember, that throughout these sessions, Aingeal Rose was not in a trance and neither was she channeling through any spiritual or psychic entity, spirit, angel or ascended master. She simply down-steps this information and knowledge directly from Source through the Akashic Records. This book contains the transcript of one of those broadcasts. The transcripts are shown in their original Question & Answer format and are conversational and colloquial in nature.

If you'd like to learn how to read the Akashic Records, check out our home-study course here: https://aingealroseandahonu.com

The Session

Aingeal Rose: Welcome to our second Akashic Records book. It was down stepped on Mother's Day, and we all know how important that beautiful Divine Mother energy is. Thank you for being with us.

Before we begin with the questions, there is something we'd like to include in this session. We had an evening in 2012 with our Akashic Records group where I was asked questions about famous people in history who had died. We called it the *Famous Deceased* and we publish some of it now as part of this series for your information.

1. **Hitler:** Hitler has not re-incarnated. He is confined on a circular orbit and is learning how God sees things. He is observing until a certain time cycle have elapsed. He can observe but not participate in earthly affairs.

2. **Joan of Arc:** She reincarnated as a Victorian child and was a normal, peaceful but gifted artist. Following her previous life of chaos, she chose a new life of peace. She said she would fight again for her principles. She is not physical now but has dictated/channeled spiritual knowledge into people. She has no desire to be in the Earth drama at this time. She was an old Atlantean.

3. **Harriet Tubman**: She is not now in body but had one incarnation as a black newspaper boy who died aged 11. She is disappointed with the mistreatment of humans despite slavery being 'officially' over. "You haven't changed that much", were her first words. "Freedom is everybody's right but must be earned, preserved and upheld," she said.

4. **John F. Kennedy**: JFK is with the group of the Founding Fathers, not in body but is close to the Earth. He has his nose in politics, actively engaged in trying to change politics to truth. He is angry about treason and lies being told to the

American people. He supports scientific development and influences policies toward peace. He is an activist in spirit.

5. **Michael Jackson**: Michael Jackson is being healed in Spirit. He was confused about his identity as a wounded being. He is taking responsibility now for his lack of responsibility then! He is not concerned with the Earth right now.

6. **Princess Diana**: Princess Diana is back. She is 3 years old at the time of this question. (This was first written in 2012.) She is in the family of Dodi Al Fayed as a grand-daughter. She has chosen this because they are an old family soul group that has Biblical roots. She used her time in the Royal household to garner influence for her new mission as a strong female presence in the Arab/Muslim world.

7. **Mary Magdalene**: She was not legally married to Jesus but they are twin souls. In that way, no legal marriage was necessary because of the twin soul relationship. They did have children and did go to France. She was not a prostitute—this story was put out by dissatisfied men that could not defile her in any other way. There is no pure blood line left today but there is a Gene Code that can allow truth. She is not on the planet now as she is too busy in spirit. Her purpose here was to re-

introduce gene codes into the human bloodline so that humans can remember God.

8. **Jesus Christ**: He is part of the same off-planet soul group as Mary Magdalene. They are involved in advanced spiritual work. They are part of promoting advancement on many star systems. He is liaison with other alien places, working for inter-dimensional peace. He is not in body now but could be seen in spirit at some future point if he deems it appropriate. He was not crucified. He was arrested then escaped as Pilate was paid off by some well-connected Essenes but not everyone knows of this. He has not embodied since then. He is aware of prayers.

9. **Blessed Mother of Jesus**: She was not a virgin. She was aged 14-15 when she married. She is a huge influence on the Earth and is a peaceful, forgiving presence. She wants to wash away the past. She was well aware of the mission of Jesus. She wants to bring peace and cares very much about humanity.

10. **Kim Jong-il:** He is happy to be out of the responsibility of Earth and happy to be with his soul family. He did not care about people and he was so glad it's over! He wants nothing to do with Earth right now.

11. **George Washington**: George Washington is not involved in current politics. He has been gone a long time. He is in a place of learning and is not in body.

12. **Gandhi**: Gandhi has ascended to a ball of light. His is a presence without form. He is holding space for peace and does not need to embody again.

13. **Queen Elizabeth 1st**: She has reincarnated as a Rock Star, somewhat like Bonnie Tyler. She is now living out of politics yet influential through her music. She is enjoying her freedom being a Rock Star, which for her is a leadership role without the responsibility. She is enjoying the self-expression in this role in this time that she could not have done as Queen Elizabeth of England.

14. **Dr. Mary Wallace**: Dr. Mary Wallace has come back. She is now a grandmother in Connecticut. She came back for home and family and community.

15. **Thomas Jefferson**: He is trying to implement a new way to trade and do business between different countries. He is active in politics working to inspire new ways of thinking. He has a lot to do with the business of money right now. He got a lot of help and support from women who unknown to others, collaborated in the writing of the Constitution.

16. **Franklin Roosevelt**: Franklin was angry and was exposed to higher learning for a long time. He is putting together writings like a treatise on history so as to keep history correct. He is setting the record straight. It is an independent work for his own sake, as he regrets some of his own decisions. His is not in body but is living through his progeny.

17. **Pat Tillman**: Pat Tillman has not returned. He has a history of being shot in battle. He knows it was a foolish choice to again join the military. It was an un-reconciled past imprint that made him join again. He is doing a rest and review right now.

18. **John Lennon**: He is coming into his own grandchild because he wants to stay close to his family. He will play music again and will influence the world again.

19. **William Wallace**: William Wallace has been back a few times, in the USA and not in his native Scotland. This was a surprise because he came back in cowboy times. He liked the freedom of the Wild West. He was a fine upstanding man who helped form the West. He wrote several books and may indeed have been Louis L'Amour. He is not in body right now.

20. **Osama bin Laden**: He has been dead over 6 years and the US Seals account is a

political fabrication. He was blamed for a lot of things he did not do. He was part of a plan to collapse society, to break down morale and to chip away at people's personal freedoms, but he did not initiate it. He would hire people for governments and was well paid. His paid followers would die in suicide missions to please Allah. He is caught in a whirlpool because so much hatred was projected towards him. It's keeping him caught in the 3rd astral layer and he will not shift until our negativity, blame and hatred is released from him.

21. **John Wayne**: John is resting peacefully in Spirit. He doesn't care that his house in Newport Beach was demolished.

22. **Thoth/Hermes**: Thoth is a shape shifter. He is on the side of the One-World agenda. He has manipulated serpent energy in the Dark Arts and has not always used his power with integrity. He actually enjoys being a trickster, giving half-truths because he believes, if you're going to be that stupid, you deserve it! He thinks humans are idiots. He plays the role of giving half-truths and enjoys seeing people struggle trying to figure it all out. He is not interested if people fall further through his mis-information and has no sympathy for our ignorance.

23. **Malcolm X**: He is not in body but rehabilitating. He is in a special group of learning where his back is to the Earth.

24. **Martin Luther King**: MLK being assassinated was an easy way out for him. He is not in body now but will come back as a religious person. He is part of the JFK group that is together because they have more impact as a spiritual group than they would as individuals here in body. He works psychically through others and has helped Barrack Obama and others by giving them brotherly strength.

25. **Abraham Lincoln**: Abraham Lincoln was taken out by people close to him in the South.

26. **Julius Caesar:** Julius Caesar has an indifferent attitude. It was a long time ago and his soul does not want him to be seen as 'that person'. He has reincarnated several times, once as a Sculptor and another as a Science Teacher. He is annoyed that he has been perceived as negative all this time when he was trying to do his best under difficult circumstances.

27. **Nicola Tesla**: Tesla is influencing the Earth in a good way. He is getting more of his inventions into use. He is inspiring inventors to bring their works to market.

28. **Napoleon Bonaparte**: Napoleon has a lot of Karma to make up for. He is living through his progeny and his progeny was affected by his Karma. It took a long time and he has learned a lot. He is being used in Spirit because he was a strong leader. He has no plans to return to the Earth plane.

29. **ANU of the Annunaki**: Is interested in what happens here, but he can't intervene.

30. **Jacques Cousteau**: Jacques Cousteau is not on the planet now yet his spirit is an integral part of preserving the oceans. He is an advanced being surrounded by music. He could come back with new information in about 3 years because of his huge concern for the oceans.

Okay, let's get started. I'm going to say the prayer and then we'll begin.

… Aingeal Rose says the prayer…

Beautiful blue light today, filling the room. It's a beautiful royal blue, which feels so peaceful and calm. I'm ready for the first question.

Question One

Q: Did Hitler really survive the 2nd World War and escape to South America?

A: I don't see Hitler living long after the war so, I say 'no' to that question.

However, in the session on *The Famous Deceased* someone asked where Hitler was, and I saw a picture similar to the rings of Saturn. It was not Saturn but a plane of existence where he was circling around and around. I was told he was not allowed to reincarnate on Earth for many cycles*.

The reason Hitler is not allowed to return to the Earth right now is to give Earth and her people an opportunity to evolve on their own without his influence. Even if Hitler chose to reincarnate as someone benign, the fact that he achieved a high leadership status means he would still be a powerful influence because of the energy around his auric field.

Because of this high degree of negative influence, he has been quarantined to a particular plane of existence in rotation where he can observe what happens on Earth. Because of this, his influence is much reduced and in some places is no more than a memory. Thus, he is being kept from incarnating here until he and the mass consciousness changes.

Source explained to us that people who end up being leaders and influencers have been building up leadership energy in their auric fields through many lifetimes.

*(Cycles are cosmic rotations in the galaxy that take many years to complete.)

Question Two

Q: Why are the higher frequency energies not able to win over the lower energies that are attempting to bring us down?

A: We need to understand that we are the ones who have to change. It is not set up where higher beings come and save us. That's not what this is about. If that was the way it was, God Source would've come in and saved us from a lot of things before now. The reason why low-frequency energies can take hold is because we still have those frequencies inside us. As much as we have light, we have shadow, and we are being asked to clear our collective shadows.

The lower forces are not winning. There is plenty of light and plenty of victories happening now. Keep your thoughts on that reality.

Ahonu and I had a conversation about how difficult it can be to love ourselves. What that means is, if somebody said to you "Do you really believe that all that is ever going to happen to you is for your good?" Would you be able to answer "Yes"?

We all deserve only goodness and that applies to everybody across the board, no matter who they are, or what they've done, or how they're behaving. Source's intention is your good and only your good. The thing is, there are parts of us that don't believe it. We may say we believe it but that isn't the truth, if we are really honest with ourselves. We are getting a lot of blessings, but that is to help us to clear out our own suppressed shadow. That's really the work.

Question Three

Q: **What can we do to change our vibration and make the world a better place?**

A: First, let me clear up the vibration issue; what you really want is to raise your *frequency,* not your vibration. Your vibration is connected to magnetics and the higher your vibration, the denser, or more magnetic, you become. What we're being asked to do is raise our *frequency,* which is *electrical.*

To raise your frequency on the 3D level, you can treat yourself with color and you can change your diet to more live and raw foods. Juicing more raw foods and bringing more life force energy into yourself will not only change the frequency of your body, but also your consciousness.

You will find that as you change your diet you feel and think differently, and are more connected to subtler energies.

You can sun-gaze by looking at the sunrise in the morning just as it is coming up for 10-20 seconds, and do the same at sunset. (More about Sun Gazing in Book 3.) This will bring the energy of the Sun into you, which is very regenerative and grounding. It is also very clarifying and centering. Make sure you drink plenty of pure water and increase your intake of good quality Vitamin C.

Meditate every day, work with your dreams and establish a relationship with your inner self through your dreams, watch your thoughts and your choices, be deliberate and conscious of your choices. Choose the highest standards of love and behavior for yourself and others.

We've talked before about increasing your standard of love for yourself in terms of what you accept in your life. This means actively saying '*no*' to habits that you may have that are self-destructive. Say '*no*' to toxic people and environments. Choose better for yourself *on all levels.* Say '*no*' to abuse of any kind and do not abuse or control others.

At the highest level, love is all there is. Create from love, and make every decision based on love. Forgiveness is huge in this time. True forgiveness means that you don't say somebody is guilty and then say you're releasing them from whatever they may have done. True forgiveness is the recognition that *at the highest level* everyone is loved the same and deserves the best of love.

Source has told us that all that happens continually in creation is that we're all given more opportunities to discover love and to *be* love.

It doesn't matter how bad you've been or what kind of crime is committed, ultimately it's all about love and forgiveness—coming to a place of harmlessness within yourself. Harmless means that you don't wish ill will on anyone. You understand that they are loved as much as you, and that what they really need is to know that. Raise your frequency by coming to a place of harmlessness for yourself and for others.

When you find yourself wanting to judge someone, catch it and remind yourself that you *can't* judge because Source doesn't judge. Remember that each person is always given another, and another, and another opportunity to find, experience and know love.

Question Four

Q: **What is the fastest way to clear your shadow self?**

A: Everything I just mentioned. The most important message about the shadow is that it can be very subtle in its manipulations. It's about monitoring yourself and that's a spiritual discipline—to be very mindful of what you're doing, thinking, choosing or not choosing.

Ahonu and I had a great discussion on our podcast (podcast.worldofempowerment.com) about guilt and how guilt can be present through your entire life. This guilt can relate back to something that may have occurred 10, 20, 30 years ago, or even eons ago. The ego will always find ways to make you guilty, and in this discussion I am equating the shadow and ego as the same thing.

Not only is it guilt toward yourself but anytime you make another person guilty you're going to feel guilt because we are brought up to believe that *guilt is judgment and judgment demands punishment.* It's just the way the psychology works within us.

Question Five

Q: There is a healing technique called *The Reconnection* developed by Dr. Eric Pearl. Is this really using the highest frequencies available on the planet?

A: Of course it's not using the highest frequencies available on the planet. Source say's we have no idea of the highest frequencies available on this planet. Dr. Pearl's method *is* using high frequencies. Ultimately, the field of Love is the highest frequency and we haven't reached that yet, not in its true essence.

Question Six

Q: Are there fleets of alien ships stationed above the Earth that we can't see?

A: A lot of the ships out there belong to our own government. We've had that technology for many years. Many of the sightings are our own military. But there are alien ships too. They don't stay constantly in our skies, coming and going, sometimes in fleets but more often in just a few numbers at once. They have the ability to cloak themselves. Some of them are in relationships with our governments and they come here to converse with military personnel on military bases. Yes, that's a surprise.

Question Seven

Q: Is the reptilian race real and are they a good or bad influence on us?

A: The reptilian race is very real and has been here a long time. They came to this planet billions of years ago when this planet fell into a lower density. They came here to colonize and live amongst other races at that time and have been here ever since.

I practice psychic surgery and I take reptiles off people all the time. They attach themselves to people's backs and use their energy.

Do they have a good or bad affect? In fairness to them, both effects are going on. You have reptilians that are considered lower life forms that live off other peoples energies, and then there are other reptilians that choose to evolve into a higher life form. So, both things going on right now.

Question Eight

Q: None of the techniques or meditations I've used work anymore. How do we defend and protect ourselves from dark energies and psychic attacks?

A: Ultimately, everything is within us. This is the mature thing we need to understand. We can look at the world today and see there are a lot more dark entities floating around than ever before. The fact is that many of those dark entities have been created by our own shadow selves that we haven't purified. This may seem like a very simple answer but since everything is within you, anything that you go through in terms of an attack, can be unraveled or diffused by you. How?

A good thing is to write about what these attacks mean to you and your thoughts and feeling about them.

To find out more about the process of Journaling I refer you to my home-study course on Transformational Writing at https://aingealroseandahonu.com. If you do this honestly you will find what the common cause is within you. On the higher level, negative forces have no power of their own, but get their power from being fed more negativity by us and our negative thoughts and feelings. They latch onto a person and feed off their negativity, compounding the problem.

Still, there has to be some common denominator between the person being attacked and the attacking energy. We need to remember that all effects are energy and can be unraveled and diffused by inquiry via journaling. Journaling unravels the energy through honestly describing our thoughts and feelings and asking ourselves what the things we are experiencing mean to us. We make associations, or conclusions, with everything we experience in life.

We create the meaning and this is what we attract to ourselves. We can undo any type of energy this way by re-defining what things mean to us and making it serve us in a positive rather than a negative way. If something seems to be coming at you from 'outside' of you, you can still become a transformer of the energy by journaling about it. We can't lie to ourselves any longer and tell ourselves that the things we're experiencing have nothing to do with us, or are outside of us.

They have everything to do with us. Everything that's going on now has everything to do with us. When I've been in very deep terror and that terror is all-consuming and I can't think correctly, I appeal to Source for help.

I will hear the voice that encourages me to choose peace instead of the terror. That suggestion is an encouragement for me to make a decision. When you're in stark terror, it's hard to believe that some part of you is choosing it instead of peace, but this is, in fact, the case. When I finally choose peace, suddenly my feelings begin to change and the fear dissolves.

Question Nine

Q: Are GM (genetically modified) crops a big problem? Are all derivatives of soy and soy extracts GM and therefore harmful?

A: There is some good non-GM soy but it is not always labeled as such. The only way you can be sure is when somebody goes to the trouble of labeling their soy product as non-GM, otherwise most soy on the market today is questionable. GM foods are harmful and should be avoided entirely where possible.

(FYI—we have been told there are many apps you can download on your iPhone or Android that allows you to scan grocery items and not only see who is making the product, but also show you if they support the labeling of GM foods.)

Question Ten

Q: Is wheat harmful to the body?

A: Most wheat is now harmful because of the pesticides and fungicides that are sprayed in the soil and on the plants. Organic, non-GM wheat may not cause the same reactions in people, so you have to watch your own body. One reason people are having reactions to these grains in general is because the soil that they're being grown in is contaminated with pesticides and fungicides. Unfortunately the wheat plant has gotten a bad name when it is really the chemicals used in growing it that is the culprit.

If you know someone who is growing organic, non-GM wheat, the chances are your body will tolerate it well. What we need to understand collectively is that all of our immune systems have been under attack for years and we're all in a weakened state.

It has a lot to do with our compromised environment and what's being done to foods. Food sensitivities build up over time until your body can't handle it anymore.

I stopped eating grains for a while and I could tell the difference in my body right away. I felt much more balanced. No grain, of course, means no bread, no cereals, no rice and no corn. You can still have breads and baked goods that are made from almond flour or coconut flour and there are lots of recipes out there for those.

Question Eleven

Q: Some say that once you eat GM food it encrypts into your DNA and that it is permanent. Can you reverse these damaging effects of GM foods?

A: What Source is saying is what's really being encrypted is a toxin. DNA can be altered and is altered all the time. It fluctuates and is not always a stable thing in us. It is affected by our emotions and how we react to things.

Because of this, I'm not seeing that GMO's cause permanent damage, but it is considered a toxin because your system must work hard to eliminate the effects of it.

If you keep eating GM foods over a long period, you could permanently damage your digestive system and your liver. Your body's own ability to fight off these damages will weaken, and the way you would normally digest food will slow down and cause progressive damage until your system won't be able to function the way it should.

This is what we really want to be aware of and avoid, because if you don't do anything and you keep eating these foods, your body will become artificial, meaning it's going to be altered genetically. So, your point is well taken in the sense of the level that these foods imprint into our system.

Source is saying we can take care of this now by buying or growing organically and by making sure farmers are also using non-GMO seeds. We're being advised to grow our own food in our own homes even if we have to put it in a window box if you don't have land, or put your crop in plastic gallon jugs.

In other words, there's ways to do this so you're not dependent on food stores until the laws are passed for GMO labeling of food.

FYI, Whole Foods Markets has come out and said that within five years they're going to have GMO labeling present on every item in their stores so you will know whether it's a GMO product or not.

This is a big movement across the world, and we're making headway with this, but until everything's labeled you have to be really selective about your food.

The other thing Source is showing me is that green light is a solution. Remember that the

Green Ray is the predominant color ray for plant life and our own biologies on this planet.

Consider visualizing green light on your body. You could also buy yourself some inexpensive theater gels, or a light box and start treating yourself with color.

If you decide to get into color therapy it will build up your immune system. Light and color is food for our bodies. We know we are made of color and sound.

Q: Why do we eat food at all?

A: It's because it contains sunlight and that's how we feed ourselves. Consider the fact that you can treat yourself with colors directly. Get yourself a good book online about color therapy that goes into detail about what different colors do and start treating yourself with colors. You'll find that you're less hungry for regular food and you'll be more discerning.

So, there are solutions to the GMO problem.

Question Twelve

Q: How is the political situation looking in the world this week?

A: I see talks going on. Leaders are meeting with leaders and for a time it looks positive. They're looking at the environment and politics and they're looking at money. Some governments are coming together to try to find a better way to live. Many genuinely desire their countries to thrive. At times they try to work out plans together and pool together against some of the big corporations that are harming the world. Others are enmeshing themselves deeper and allowing themselves to be controlled by the corporate culture. However, I'm seeing a lot of conversations going on that feels positive.

Question Thirteen

Q: Will the Boston bombings be exposed as an inside job meant to misguide the public?

A: What you are really asking is: were the Boston bombings a terrorist attack or was it orchestrated by our own government?

While we always sympathize with those genuinely hurt in any kind of attack, there have been occasions in the past when *some* orchestration took place. Many of these incidents unfortunately are used to get people familiar with seeing troops in the streets and implementing a taste of martial law. In the small community in Boston they succeeded in easily controlling the neighborhood.

Question Fourteen

Q: Will black ops like Area 51 be uncovered and exposed to the public anytime soon?

A: Area 51 is an area in Nevada that is heavily guarded. There's been reports of extraterrestrial activity and advanced military practices going on there. So, the question is, will that area be exposed and uncovered so that the public can know what's going on there? I don't see it being uncovered anytime soon. We really have to understand, when we ask these kinds of questions, that our government and military are not interested in admitting anything.

If Area 51 was to be exposed, it would be through other people who are getting footage of the area or by someone who worked there. There has already been information about Area 51 released in this way. I don't see the government being willing to admit anything about it anytime soon.

Question Fifteen

Q: What do you see for the economy?

A: Right now there is some recovery going on and some things are getting better in places. I'm giving credit to the particular states or cities where things are better. It doesn't look like it's because of any sort of government changes—rather it is because of state changes. Things look like they are recovering, even though what I'm also hearing is we're still in very fluctuating times where things can go in any direction.

Question Sixteen

Q: What is the energy of China? Does it have good intentions for the USA and the world or not?

A: First and foremost, China has good intentions for itself. China is very concerned with his own people and with its own progress. Does it have a plan to buy up a lot of the United States? On one level they just think it is good business to accumulate acquisitions. They are also cooperating with other governments concerning the environment and for solutions to other problems globally. I don't see that China has a plan right now to take over the world, or the USA: It is mostly concerned with its own country and feeding its own population and acquiring assets along the way. That's the way it looks right now, but as we know, things change.

Question Seventeen

Q: Is Nigel Farage making headway in awakening Europeans towards more freedom and independence?

A: Yes, he is. Nigel has been a member of the European Parliament for South East England and co-chairs a freedom and democracy group. He's an advocate for freedom and justice. He has been instrumental in getting many more people on board with important issues and has made a lot of headway and has many allies now.

Question Eighteen

Q: Do you see masses rising up uniting and refusing to pay taxes?

A: People are more concerned with survival and their income. They're concerned about their families and keeping their homes. They're concerned about health and the rising cost of food. This is where the predominant energy is in terms of what people really care about right now. I don't see the masses rising up about any of these things either.

They will care about taxes eventually when systems collapse and things get redefined but even with that, I don't see that we'll ever have no tax. As I look down the road, I still see taxes but they're more fair and I don't see masses of people revolting against taxes anytime soon.

Question Nineteen

Q: There is a supposed super soldier called James Casbolt (Michael Prince) spreading fear right now. He talks about super soldiers being built who are indestructible and who will work to subdue the population and create concentration camps all over the world. Are his statements true or is he just trying to instigate fear?

A: There exists technology for super soldiers and war is its motive. They have been working on prototypes for a while. Some are ready for use, but I don't see them in large numbers yet, even though the technology is there.

They will use them as replacements for living soldiers. They want to see how far they can go with robotic technology. As with the development of drones, the same thing is happening with the super-soldiers.

Some aggressive governments want super-soldiers to replace human soldiers and be much more powerful, difficult to destroy, and who will kill without a conscience. It is another level of the war-game technology.

In terms of subduing the population, I don't see that as the main motive but, of course, they could use these soldiers for anything they wish. But right now, they're being made predominantly for war.

Let me address the whole subduing the population issue and ask Source about that, because it looks like (at least this week) things are shifting in a positive way. We're going to see more and more governments working toward a harmonious Earth. Some governments are withdrawing from this paradigm of domination and control and are becoming more interested in the health and welfare of their populations and of the Earth in general. I don't see America following suit yet, however, but hopefully it will.

It's not a *worldwide* agreement anymore to suppress and control populations. There has been a turn toward people caring about the Earth and I find that really wonderful, actually. The dark energies are still playing their games, yes, but it doesn't look like they're going to be able to pull off their population control plans everywhere.

Question Twenty

Q: According to Ainslie MacLeod, there are 10 Soul levels. Does Source agree?

A: Source says don't define yourselves by absolutes. It guides us to be careful with belief systems that are finite or absolute because we and the universe are much greater and more malleable than that.

We have many *layers* and many higher and lower aspects. We are designed for infinity because we're all part of an ever-expanding creation. The soul is built upon experiences of the individuated spirit as it journeys through creation. As creation expands, it expands the potential for us and the universe. This happens in every moment.

Ainslie MacLeod is aware of certain frequency levels but if any person hasn't seen past 10 frequency bands it just means they haven't seen past them, and maybe they're not ready to.

Question

Twenty One

Q: Does gas fracking cause irreparable damage to the Earth?

A: Yes, it causes damage in the short and long term. If you could see under the Earth you'd see where the soil is collapsing, where there's huge pockets of methane gas building up, where there's more fissures and cracks throughout the ocean floor and throughout the upper geological layers of our planet.

The Earth has already been damaged by human activity. Fracking adds to that trauma. The Earth is adjusting herself and ultimately the Earth will change. Once that change is finished the Earth will once again stabilize.

Currently the Earth is in a process of collapsing underneath in many places. You may hear about more sinkholes and loud booms—these are indications of shifts going on causing many to fear the future.

Question

Twenty Two

Q: If everything happens at once and time is not linear, are all my lives 'me' in the same soul?

A: Yes, they're all you as one soul.

Here's a story to make the point: I was in a meditation years ago and I was taken to a plane of existence where there was a female in the front of a classroom teaching hundreds of people. I immediately recognized her as myself teaching all these other aspects of myself. There were various nationalities there, both sexes, young and old in the room. I knew they were all 'me' because the core vibration of each of them was the same as me even though they all looked different.

Ahonu reports that in a quantum jump to a different dimensional space, he saw thousands of himself going off in multitudes of directions from where he stood, every one of them anchored in a particular experience of time in that moment.

So yes, they are all you and are all part of your soul. They all affect you and vice versa.

Question

Twenty Three

Q: Was Jesus really crucified?

A: No, many were crucified but that Being escaped to France with Pilate's help and went on to have five children. Pontius Pilate was bribed by some of Jesus' followers, helping Jesus escape by looking the other way. There is a lot more to this story, but perhaps at another time or in another book of Answers From The Akashic Records.

Question Twenty Four

Q: Do any people embody Jesus' soul?

A: If you are talking about the person Jesus, no. People don't embody his soul. Jesus was here to put the Christ consciousness potential into the planetary grids and into the human bloodlines. It was not just for *certain* families, but for *all* humanity. Now, *everyone* has these codes within them. That is what he did and what he achieved.

As a result, we all have the potential for Christ consciousness not only for the planet, but for ourselves.

Question

Twenty Five

Q: Many children are committing crime and even murder. How do we protect our families and our children from them?

A: We need to remember that everybody has a holy Guardian Angel appointed to them and everybody has their own soul contract, including children. What people do makes sense on some level if you understood what was going on with them as a soul.

To help violent children, love and prayers make a difference. Invoke their Angel to be by their side. You can do a lot by the thoughts you send a person, by the visualizations you send. What we offer each other energetically makes a difference.

To protect yourself and your children, picture your family surrounded in beautiful light when you go to sleep at night. Talk to them mentally and remember that communication is non-local.

You can help avert danger by taking the time to surround those you love in a protective light.

I remember a story a woman told about her husband years ago. She had gotten into an argument with him as he was leaving that evening to go on a flight for business. When he left she was not in a good frame of mind, fostering negative thoughts about him. When she realized she was thinking negatively about him she decided to shift her thoughts and send him a blessing instead. When her husband arrived at his destination he called his wife and told her that the plane had gone through a period where it was in trouble and it was uncertain whether they were going to make it.

He then told her that all of a sudden everything shifted and all was well. The wife made the correlation in her own mind, that when she was thinking ill towards her husband, it corresponded to the time his plane was in jeopardy. The plane righted itself exactly at the time she shifted her negative thoughts to a blessing. She believed her thoughts had that much influence over the events in her husband's life.

Here's another example to make the point of how our thoughts affect others for good or ill. When I was in Chicago years ago, I was getting in an elevator and met a young man who was maybe 25 years old. He was the only person on the elevator with me. He had on a wool coat that was really nice except the coat was too big for him.

In my mind, as I was looking at him, I was thinking,

Wow, really nice coat dude but it's too big on you.

Just as I thought that, he got uncomfortable and started looking down at his coat and adjusting it.

I caught it right away that my thoughts had made him self-conscious. So, I changed my thoughts right then and there and in my mind I said I was sorry, and what a beautiful coat he was wearing, and how great it looked on him. Just then, he stood up straight and tall and it caused a completely different reaction in him. We have tremendous power over what happens.

So, when you ask about protecting your children, remember you have a lot of power to influence and support people positively. It is something we need to do even more in these times.

Question

Twenty Six

Q: What can you tell us about autistic children?

A: These children actually come from a plane of existence that is very advanced, much like the Indigos. Many of them have a contract to be autistic. Of course, their *spirit* is not autistic; rather they choose to have an autistic experience.

Specifically, the autistic children are teaching us about the poisons of vaccines and about the poisons in foods. They need to be on a predominantly organic diet without grains. They require chemical-free foods. Their purpose is to teach us a different way to communicate with each other. They are here to support telepathic communication and emotional communication so that we can get to deeper levels of ourselves. These spirits subject themselves to the toxins that cause them to be autistic in order to fulfill that contract.

The other part is they are teaching us about the sensitivities to foods so that we have to choose foods that are organic and unprocessed and also bring to the fore some corrupt purveyors of vaccinations.

Many of these advanced children, whether they're autistic, indigo or crystal, are here to help move us into a more light-based way to live, and that means more pure color, more pure foods and more pure environment.

I see royal blue around these children because they function at a different frequency band. I have spoken to a lot of parents who have reversed many of the effects in their autistic children by changing to a pure diet and incorporating some energetic and elevated music therapies into their lives.

As for celiac disease, we are still talking about the body's reaction to poisons and unnatural fungi.

Question
Twenty Seven

Q: How can I tell that I'm living in the right place?

A: You can know intuitively by simply asking yourself and wait and feel for the answer. A good place for you is a place that feels nourishing, where you feel joyful, where you feel a sense of peace being there. It is so important to be in the place that feels right for you.

That's how I always tell if a place is right for me—if I feel nourished by the land in the area, if I feel happy being there, then I stay. If it supports a feeling of expansiveness for me for what I'm going to do, my work, my personal growth, then I stay. That's how I tell if I'm in the right place.

Ask yourself, does the place you're in support that? Alternatively, you could ask your own Akashic Records.

Question

Twenty Eight

Q: What happened to Amelia Earhart?

A: Her plane went down in a small forested area near an island. She was with a man and there was a mechanical failure of her aircraft. I can see the needles on the dials getting stuck and I see her going down among the trees.

Question

Twenty Nine

Q: What can you tell us about Kiesha Crowther, the Little Grandmother? Is she an authentic representative of Truth?

A: She feels spiritually appointed to do the work she's doing and 90% of what she says seems to be valid.

Question Thirty

Q: Are any main news medias positive or truthful?

A: I don't see any of them able to really come out and tell the truth about many of the things happening in our world. It looks like both propaganda and censorship is rife across the board.

Question

Thirty One

Q: Is hair loss reversible?

A: Hair loss has to do with the amount of keratin in the skin. The head is part of the organ of the skin and hair loss has to do with the elasticity of the skin. When the elasticity begins to change, the cells in the skin start to change and they don't support certain things in certain parts of the body any longer. People don't only lose hair on their heads; they lose hair on their arms and on their legs, too.

Is hair loss reversible? Once again I'm seeing a color—it's a combination of royal blue and violet blue light. This light stimulates hair growth. Hair loss is also connected to hormone levels. The skin itself does a lot to filter out toxins—it is a protector from the environment and it will close down if it is overloaded or if the environment is too toxic.

When that happens, you'll see that people will lose hair or will have less hair on their bodies. You can also look into your hormone levels and see if they are balanced. So, hair loss is reversible but it depends on what the damages is to your own system. Ahonu did 2 short YouTube videos on hair: *Head Shave, Anyone?* https://youtu.be/MHVqsrhCa9U and *Hair, One Family's Experience*—https://youtu.be/tYj4y_RjVwg

Question

Thirty Two

Q: Can gray hair be reversed?

A: Gray hair has to do with aging and hormone levels which is a gradual progression. It could be reversed if you can do some work on the chemical and hormone imbalances inside your body. Eating more live foods sometimes reverses graying hair.

Question

Thirty Three

Q: **Will big chains stores survive or collapse in the next 10 years?**

A: Right now they have a big momentum because so many people use these stores. They'll always cater to the mass market and adapt to follow the consumer demand. Some will supply healthier products as demand changes, others will supply the cheapest and the most toxic of foods and still continue in business because of their price points. Either way, I don't see the principle of big chain stores collapsing.

The Profundities

Summary of Akashic Records Session

1. If the place you live supports you, you are in the right place.
2. The reason why low-frequency energies can take hold is because we still have those frequencies inside of us.
3. There is plenty of light and plenty of victories happening now and we need to keep our thoughts on that reality.
4. There is a part of us that doesn't believe that Source loves us.
5. Some governments are genuinely trying to find the right way to live and for their countries to thrive.
6. Some governments are withdrawing from the paradigm of domination and control and are becoming more interested in the health and welfare of their populations and of the Earth in general.
7. It's not a worldwide agreement anymore to suppress and control populations.
8. The real reason people are having reactions to grains in general is because the soil that they're being grown in is contaminated with pesticides and fungicides.
9. All of our immune systems have been under attack for quite a few years now and we're all in a weakened state.
10. DNA can be altered and is altered all the time.
11. GMOs are being encrypted into the body as a toxin.
12. Remember that the Green Ray is the predominant color ray for plant life and our own biology on this planet.
13. We have no idea of the highest frequencies available on this planet.
14. Many advanced children, whether they're autistic, indigo or crystal, are here to help move us into a more light-based way to live, and that means more pure color, more pure foods and more pure environment.
15. Everyone has Christ consciousness codes within them.
16. When you're in stark terror, it's hard to believe that some part of you is choosing it instead of peace, but this is, in fact, the case.
17. Negative forces have no power of their own, but get their power from being fed more negative thoughts, feelings and fears by us.

18. All effects are energy and can be unraveled and diffused by journaling.
19. We make associations, or conclusions, with everything we experience in life.
20. We can undo any energy by re-defining what things mean to us and making it serve us in a positive rather than a negative way.
21. Everything that's going on now has everything to do with us.
22. Source says:
    - Meditate every day.
    - Work with your dreams and establish a relationship with your inner self through them.
    - Watch your thoughts.
    - Be deliberate and conscious of your choices.
    - Choose the highest standards of love and behavior for yourself and others.
    - Say 'no' to habits that are self-destructive.
    - Say 'no' to toxic people and environments.
    - Choose better for yourself on all levels.
    - Say 'no' to abuse of any kind and do not abuse or control others.
    - Raise your frequency by coming to a place of harmlessness for yourself and for others.
    - Remind yourself that you can't judge because Source doesn't judge.
    - Remember that each person is always given another and another and another opportunity to find out about love.
    - Remember that the shadow self is sinister and can be very subtle in its manipulations.
    - Be very mindful of what you're thinking, doing, choosing or not choosing.
    - Call in your I Am Presence into your body.
    - Create from love knowing that your every decision is based on love.
    - Know that we're all given more opportunities to discover love and to be love.
    - Everyone has a holy Guardian Angel appointed to them.
    - Everyone is living out their own soul contract.

- When you go to sleep at night, picture your family and children surrounded in beautiful balls of light and invoke their Angel to be by their side.
- Remember we do have a lot of power to influence and support people positively.

To get these profound statements from the Akashic Records in your mailbox, visit: https://worldofempowerment.com

Acknowledgements

Many of you have opened your hearts and minds, willing to be co-creators of a new world—a world based on love, cooperation, harmony and peace. We've had the good fortune to meet and interview many of you, all dedicated to the empowerment and awakening of humankind. We witnessed your most intimate thoughts and feelings, your fears and your strengths.

So, it is for you we have published this series of 100 books, *Answers From The Akashic Records.* You're willingness and thirst for truth has fueled a growth of awareness, allowing for the experience of wisdom and knowledge for all.

Without you, these books would not have emerged and we are grateful for the privilege of sharing these experiences with others!

Blessings!

Aingeal Rose and Ahonu

Aingeal Rose & Ahonu

WE Coach ~ WE Create ~ WE Design ~ WE Publish ~ WE Teach ~ WE EMPOWER!

With over 60 years combined experience, Twin Flames Aingeal Rose & Ahonu help you with
✔ Powerful coaching, webinars, readings
✔ Potent courses, books and podcasts designed for your ...
✔ Clarity
✔ Freedom
✔ Your conscious personal growth and
✔ Your conscious business success!

Aingeal Rose (USA) & Ahonu (Ireland) are authors, artists, publishers, speakers, researchers, ministers, radio hosts and spiritual teachers who, individually and as a Twin-Flame husband-and-wife team, have helped countless people all over the world move from mediocrity to joy, clarity and awareness through their simple but highly effective series of books, programs, workshops and online sessions.
They are trusted by clients around the world for their authentic down-to-Earth approach, and are known for empowering their clients and helping to raise the consciousness of the world.
Ahonu & Aingeal Rose are also popular media guests and co-hosts of a weekly broadcast on World of Empowerment Radio (https://podcast.worldofempowerment.com). In addition, they are ordained ministers in the non-denominational Alliance of Divine Love Ministry, bringing that devotion into everything they do.

In Sedona, AZ, they offer a memorable and joyful wedding ceremony for couples desiring a celebration that strengthens the Divine masculine and feminine bonds between them.

Aingeal Rose & Ahonu work throughout the United States and Ireland, are Master Tarot Teachers, an authority on the Akashic Records and hold certifications in Psychic Laser Therapy, Kathara Healing, Soul Retrieval, Reiki and Cellular Re-Patterning. International workshops include Twin Flames & Soul Mates, Psychic Laser Therapy, Akashic Records Training, Experiencing the Dimensional Split, Manifesting, Beginner through Advanced Tarot, Quantum Jumping, Journaling, Writing, Publishing, Visionary Art and more.

Join them, so you too can live, love and experience personal sovereignty and business success through a delightful growth of awareness delivered personally and securely by us to you through this portal to personal power! Feel the awareness and expansion of consciousness that has transformed 1,000s! Take courses on Self-Expansion or Personal Sovereignty. Find your Twin Flame or experience Dimensional Diving, all here, now!

For further information or to arrange an interview, book signing, speaking engagement, book a workshop, Spirit of Love painting or Akashic Records consultation, contact them on https://aingealroseandahonu.com or by Phone USA: +1-224-588-8026 or Skype: ah-hon-u

ahonu@ahonu.com

aingealrose@aingealrose.com

More to Explore

Thanks for reading! If you enjoyed this book or found it useful, we'd be grateful if you'd post a short review on Amazon.

Here are more of our works for you to explore:

AINGEAL ROSE & AHONU PODCAST
Twin Flame hosts of the World of Empowerment Series, Ahonu & Aingeal Rose are the creators of this consciously aware community of like-minded listeners co-creating a new world of self-mastery and love of all life everywhere! This podcast is a self-expansion experience! Listen to the archives at https://podcast.worldofempowerment.com or subscribe on iTunes here: http://apple.co/2j9kaFT

AKASHIC RECORDS—Online Group Sessions
Held on the 1st Sunday of every month online, these group Akashic Record sessions allow you to bring your big questions to Source. For spiritual/universal/global inquiries of the Universe, not for personal questions. More info here https://worldofempowerment.com

AKASHIC RECORDS TRAINING
Accelerate your spiritual knowledge by learning to read the Akashic Records so you can become an Akashic Records reader. Use the insight and knowledge for your own, your family or become a practitioner. This training is held in the USA and in Ireland—also available online at https://aingealroseandahonu.com.

TRANSFORMATIONAL WRITING
This online class will free you from many unwanted belief systems and return your own power to you. By exploring your own consciousness, you will bring many beliefs to light and put yourself in the driver's seat of choice once again. This is a powerful class using a simple tool that is yours forever. Enroll here: https://aingealroseandahonu.com

SPIRIT ART
Explore your own Inner Self through art! YOU NEED NO ART EXPERIENCE for this class! AHONU guides you through various fun-filled exercises that stimulate your intuitive self and inner child to paint! This class is fun, spiritually revealing and highly transformative. Only in Sedona, AZ - Not available online. All Materials Provided.

TWIN FLAME / SOUL MATE WORKSHOPS
How do you know if you have met your Twin Flame or a Soul Mate? What are the signs? What is their purpose? Are you in a Twin Flame relationship? What are the challenges and rewards? Includes our Twin Flames & Soul Mates eBook. These workshops answer these questions and more. USA, Ireland, online and eBook.

THE 8 STEPS TO FREEDOM
This program was originally 8 weeks, starting on the 8 day of the 8 month at 8pm for 88 minutes—it was suspended during the pandemic, and may now be back online (http://8-steps-to-freedom.com) to take at your leisure! AHONU & Aingeal Rose online deliver life-transforming outcomes, make sense of your life, understand your relationships, accelerate your possibilities and help you grow in peace and wisdom. Developed by AHONU & Aingeal Rose to fulfill specific outcomes people need, help deliver specific results people want and to solve specific challenges people have.

Other Books by
Aingeal Rose & Ahonu

Aingeal Rose & Ahonu are publishing more books all the time. Get notified by signing up for book alerts here: https://aingealroseandahonu.com

On the Web, search for AHONU or AINGEAL ROSE

A Time of Change: https://amzn.to/3cSggNE
Acupuncture: https://amzn.to/2NPsafp
Advanced Tarot Spreads: https://amzn.to/3diJLKt
Ahonu Soul Portraits: https://amzn.to/2NSZZfA
All books by Aingeal Rose: https://links.ahonu.com/all-books-by-aranda
Answers From The Akashic Records 1-100: https://links.ahonu.com/aftar
Aromatherapy: https://amzn.to/2zz4M2B
Ayurveda: https://amzn.to/2NQzWpp
Clockwork Purple Vols 1-3: https://amzn.to/2MelPtc
End Procrastination Forever: https://amzn.to/3HB0Qgk
Indigo Children: https://amzn.to/2zFbDaM
Love, Miracles & Original Creation: https://amzn.to/39FUg9H
Reiki: https://amzn.to/2NPYbE2
Tarot for Beginners: https://links.ahonu.com/tarot
The Angel Of The Forest: Search on Amazon
The Reincarnation of Columbus: http://amzn.to/291rTAc
The Nature of Reality: http://amzn.to/29dRqMt
Twin Flames & Soul Mates: https://amzn.to/2NL7Mfc
Why Did He Die? https://amzn.to/3ov4Qa8
Witches, Crows, Owls & Cats: https://amzn.to/2q6PygP

Connect With
Aingeal Rose & Ahonu

YOUTUBE: youtube.com/user/ahonuandaingealrose
TWITTER: twitter.com/ahonu
PINTEREST: pinterest.com/aingealrose/
FACEBOOK: facebook.com/aingealroseandahonu
LINKEDIN: linkedin.com/in/kevinogrady

Aingeal Rose: aingealrose.com
Q: ahonu.com
Holistic Ireland: holistic.ie
Twin Flame Productions: TwinFlameProductions.us
Sacred Earth Waters: SacredEarthWaters.com
World of Empowerment: WorldofEmpowerment.com

Ahonu.com, AingealRose.com,
WorldofEmpowerment.com

AINGEAL ROSE & AHONU

Disclaimer

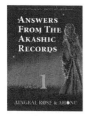

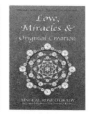

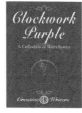

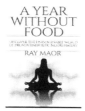
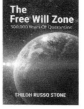

Healing
From Grief

A 3-Book Series

Why Did He Die?

The Reincarnation of Columbus

The Angel Of The Forest

by Kevin O'Grady (Ahonu)

Published by Twin Flame Productions https://twinflameproductions.us

Made in the USA
Coppell, TX
06 June 2023

17763958R10048